from my Father my son

the re-birth of a black warrior

poems by Steven Lyons

ISBN: 979-8-9912245-0-5   Paperback
ISBN: 979-8-9912245-1-2   eBook

Library of Congress Control Number: 2024920237
Book design by Glen Edelstein, Hudson Valley Book Design

First printing edition 2024

Advanced Praise for
from my Father to my son

"In a culture that is often quick to judge and slow to contemplate layers of truth and understanding, poetry forces us to think deeper, stretching our imaginations and challenging our preconceptions. In this collection, Steven Lyons offers poems that lead us to such a place and to consider the souls of others within the current cultural conversation over race."

Dr. David King, Associate Professor of Social Work, Indiana Wesleyan University

"Steven beautifully weaves together the threads of his personal journey, offering readers a poignant and powerful reflection on identity, heritage, and legacy. He navigates the complexities of race, masculinity, and familial bonds with grace and vulnerability. As he shares intimate moments and pivotal experiences, readers can't help but be moved by his courage and determination to carve out his own path while honoring the legacy of those who came before him. He does this by tapping into universal themes of love, loss, and resilience."

Sheila Fortson, Founder/Executive Director, FAME Center, Chicago, IL

Dedicated to

Janet…God's perfect, gracious gift, who embraced the realization that she was marrying an artist – a flawed one – and continues to embrace me into our 38th year.

In memory of

*Christian David (1962-2022), Julie Lyons (1941-2024),
and Daniel Myatt (1965-2024) …whose music
and words breached my soul.*

The thoughts of the son ran thus: "My hopes painted
beautiful pictures, but they are fading one by one."
Then his Father spoke to him: "Thy hopes painted pictures?
Destroy all those pictures. To watch them slowly fading is
weakening to the soul. Dare then to destroy them. Thou
canst if thou wilt. Thou must if thou wouldest be My
warrior son. I will give thee other pictures instead of those
thy hopes painted. Look up, O thou son of My love."

—Amy Carmichael, *His Thoughts Said...His Father Said*

No one engaged in warfare entangles himself with the
affairs of this life, that he may please him who enlisted him
as a soldier.

—2 Timothy 2:4 (NKJV)

For the weapons of our warfare are not of the flesh but have
divine power to destroy strongholds.

—2 Corinthians 10:4 (ESV)

contents

acknowledgements

With gratefulness to God for the influence of these authors:

Those of yesterday...

James Baldwin
Jerry Bridges
Amy Carmichael
Charles W. Chesnutt
Countee Cullen
Paul Laurence Dunbar
Elisabeth Elliot
Ralph Ellison
Langston Hughes
James Weldon Johnson
Nella Larsen
Claude McKay
Watchman Nee
Martha Snell Nicholson
Charles Spurgeon
Ida B. Wells
John A. Williams
Richard Wright

Those of today...

Ruth Haley Barton
Evan Carton
John Mark Comer
J. Alasdair Groves
Skye Jethani
Jamaica Kincaid
Toni Morrison
Barack Obama
Kevin Powell
James Haywood Rolling, Jr.
Clint Smith
Bill Thrasher
Natasha Trethewey
Paul David Tripp
Rich Villodas
Edward T. Welch
Jim Wilder
Isabel Wilkerson

And for the courage of these pioneers: John Lewis and Steve Saint, who stepped into risky spaces to create community.

And for the love of these fathers: Clint Cox, Eric Stevenson, Gustave "Gus" Tucker, Matthew Lyons, and Paul Morrison, who have sons they love sacrificially, and who have gone to battle for me at different times and in different ways.

And for the perseverance of my parents: Robert A. Lyons and Myrdice A. Lyons, who taught me that black is as beautiful as any other color.

foreword

Brian Holt

It's not hyperbole to say that Steven Lyons is one of my favorite people. I know that pastors, like parents, aren't supposed to have favorites. But we do. And Steven is one of mine.

I first met Steven more than a decade ago at a church near the city of Chicago. I was new to the city and still learning and growing as a young pastor. We became quick friends and shared many deep, meaningful conversations over the years. One of the more amusing seasons of my life came when Steven, pursuing a Master of Arts in Spiritual Formation and Discipleship, found himself in need of a pastoral internship. Despite our maturity gap, he chose me. He's gracious even to this day when he speaks of it.

We've counseled others together. We've visited infirm church members at homes and hospitals. We've prayed together at length. We've studied the Word of God together. We've pushed one another outside of our comfort zones. We've listened to each other's stories. We are brothers in Christ.

And Steven has stories worth listening to.

He possesses both a gracious spirit and the soul of a beat poet. His life experiences should have made him bitter and angry, but instead they have made him humble and introspective. I know these poems intersect with painful places from his past and present and that they may push on issues of cultural context that make you uncomfortable. I hope they do. As valuable as these words may be, they have come at a great cost.

So, I implore you, listen to Steven. He speaks softly, but with thunderous wisdom. I pray his words resonate with and challenge you—the same way they have for me many times.

2 Chronicles 20:21-22 (CSB)

Then he consulted with the people and appointed some to sing for the LORD and some to praise the splendor of his holiness. When they went out in front of the armed forces, they kept singing:

Give thanks to the LORD,
for his faithful love endures forever.

The moment they began their shouts and praises, the LORD set an ambush against the Ammonites, Moabites, and the inhabitants of Mount Seir who came to fight against Judah, and they were defeated.

Intro
Elegy Exhaled

Born: _____
Died: February 26, 2012
Interment: Today

Today I bury my son. I watched, heard, and felt him die. When the person who shot a bullet into Trayvon Martin's chest was portrayed as merely law abiding, I no longer wanted a son.

Join me at the repast; glimpse into my grief; share a recipe and a remembrance, while the music plays my soul bare. Listen as melancholia and memories alternate, coincide, color each other. Endure as I exhale the relief of having no son to fight for.

On a living room carpet is where my earthly father taught me *not to fight*. Now I understand: he simply wanted me to live. On a carpetless floor is where my Heavenly Father is teaching me *how to fight*. Now I understand: He simply wants me to die. So I may truly live.

On a carpet of contingencies is where I bargain for weapons and armor to survive. Now I understand: there are other funeral parlors, where my presence matters to someone who is simply looking for a place to sit.

———

Where is the son who will sit on the carpet as I tell of the time his grandma fainted in the grocery store? How I was scared and helpless seeing her sprawled on the ground near the checkout – even though she assured me through her chipped-tooth smile that she was fine…

…and how I could tell that no one knew what to do with the little black-yellow boy, and how I can't recall how I got home or what happened to the groceries. And how Providence protected me from predators in the aisles.

———

Where is the son who will listen as I tell of the time his grandpa fainted at the cookout? How I was scared and defenseless seeing his dignity sprawled on the grass near a tree – even though nobody heard the thud and he never actually lost consciousness…

…and how I internalized the discomfort and self-disappointment as his friends who were white kept winning at horseshoes, and how I could tell that none of the unfriendly smiling faces cared whether the little black-yellow boy at his side would grow up and faint, as long as he did not fight. And how Providence protected me as I pondered the price of performance.

━

Like birds soaring without pretense because they know there is enough sky to share, I learned to see sunbeams. But the accumulation of lessons does not always crowd out lies. Would I have told my son the truth? That his daddy fainted four times:

Once at a picnic, celebrating the end of fifth grade, the propulsion into middle school. Twice at church – different churches, years apart. And once on public transportation, delaying everyone's commute.

3

What still makes me dizzy? Fretting over who would have taught you how to throw, since your daddy's eighth-grade report card blurted "needs to work on throwing arm." And I felt bad that your grandpa felt responsible, but never found the time to make sure the grade improved.

The embarrassment of hiding in right field is nothing compared to the absence of anyone at the plate, in the stands, in the dugout, in the trenches. Except for my Father. My Father who never faints, whose understanding is unsearchable, and who gives strength to those feeling faint.

So what if my son became a fainter like his father. I would be there to hit a ball to right field, no matter how many times I struck out. I am here now. Swinging bats. Dodging bullets. Accepting the loss. But relishing in the gain from what my Father went through to have me.

My Father. Who was willing to *do* what I was unwilling to *risk*. To lose His Son. And out of love resurrect Him. Out of love for those in arms against Him. Those like me. A transformative love that fights the lies. The lie that the battle is mine. The lie that there are no sons left to fight for.

Verse 1

finding history

Progress

Listen, son…hoodies off limits
Re-read the fourteenth amendment
Nowhere that right to be found

See, son…no court could create two fifths of you
Re-read the hundred thirty-ninth psalm
The wonder that is you shall astound

Gaze squinting at the amber-less waves of asphalt trees
Count the voting booths separating you but equal the time
Gnarled knuckles unfolded to point "dar he"

Listen, son…use vernacular with caution
Recite the proverbs passed on to me
by voices confusing corners with crime zones

See, I too am a son…
ashamed to be glad you're not born to see
glad to be ashamed of what I see torn

Lives like crops unfertilized
Campaigns crafted upwind of the decay
Beneath clouds concealing crosswalks to freedom unborn

But Daddy, my ears are getting cold

Note: "Dar he" were the words Moses Wright spoke when he stood in court and identified the men who abducted his nephew, Emmett Till.

Conversation Starters

Your face resembles Emmett Till's
       Hole in the head
       No eyes in the socket
       River-soaked skin – lost count of the days
How did that happen to your face?
Tell me your story
I really want to hear if such pain can be endured

Your heart resembles mine
       Head hardened by sin
       Eyes shut to the sunlight
       Blood-cleansed skin – lost count of the cost
How did you happen to turn your back?
Tell me your story
I really want to hear if our fate can be secured

I promise not to compare
I determine not to stare
I vow to listen with both ears
I commit to be touched by your tears
       On my shoulder
       Not just handing you a tissue
Though I suppose that would be a start

Curaray Calling

Stop caring stop crying stop craving stop trying
Buried alive but needing to die
Indelible images of unrepentant warriors
Sinking into their cemetery
Where I am too quick to go – no
Instead visit the altar I built where all was surrendered
The exchange remembered
My filth Your spotlessness
My treason Your loyalty
My abandonment Your carrying
Yes – to the Cross I go

See my dirty palms from digging
See Your bleeding palms from dying
That I might bathe
Knowing my feet will be soiled from walking
Around the tombstones and dwelling too long at the wrong
        ones
Though even the path to my own is dirty
And so You wash my feet?
May it never be
Always be
Let it be
The glory I seek blossomed under that tree
The one I thought cursed

After I nursed
The wounds that would have healed
By kneeling and serving
Amidst storm clouds softening the ground
Making it harder to walk
Still carried lifeless and alive in Your embrace
If only empty handed so I could hold You tighter
The idol falls at last and the stones are hurled and I turn
To see my Savior bruised
Caring crying pleading dying
Living for me to stop lying

To start caring and keep crying
To keep cleaving and keep dying
Slaying the flesh the untruths the unbelief the underneath
The skin yet unstripped of unforgiveness
Until I behold Love
Speared sharper
Stretched deeper and higher and wider
Than the grave I've been digging
Than the pit You reached in
To send me soaring

How humbling now trembling
Flying again above the river
Where the bodies splashed and bled
Floated and sank into grace
Though buried years before

While I crash from trying to pilot instead of praise
Yet from the wreckage
You save me with a Word
You keep raising me to the treehouse
Where the view reveals how much
You care

Note: Curaray is the river where the martyred bodies of missionaries Jim Elliot, Pete Fleming, Ed McCully, Nate Saint, and Roger Youderian were discovered. Descendants of Nate Saint were baptized there.

Freedom (of) Summer

It's the humidity that's so oppressive
Each droplet holding a day's worth of misgivings
Non-discriminating, non-incriminating dew
Settling on black and white brows the same
As they work together to look past and inside of
Each other

And this ain't even Mississippi
Where shirts were drenched by more than armpits
Sinus headaches make their mark in the Midwest
An invention of collective failures
Collective longings and unbelongings all traced to fear of
Each other

Little black boy in the summer of being two
The year of the three murders
His backyard pool was already desegregated
His parents made sure
To march in the north by educating the ouches out of
Each other

And he grew up noticing neither humidity nor central air
And he played with his white friends
Until accusations replaced innocence
Fingers when pointed still throw but can't catch

Until they're extended enough to start praying:

"Am I the each or the other?"

Note: Freedom Summer was a project in Mississippi in 1964, organized by leadership from the Student Nonviolent Coordinating Committee, to help enfranchise black citizens. The first three volunteers to arrive – James Chaney, Andrew Goodman, and Michael Schwerner – were murdered.

redemption wins

you're standing in a garden clothed waist-high in wildflowers
(stay with me now)
humming notes that roll across a pre-Greensleeves meadow
to a First-born manger
in nature's walk-in closet you can examine
things private things public things getting sunburnt in the shade

what if you're given lenses
that transition to recognize when camouflage conceals
freshly calloused skin that catches whatever it rubs
finding itself betrothed to thoughts and dreams
of a civilization where gardens can't grow

notice the raindrop
denied its destiny to form a lake between branches
where two caterpillars could have kicked back conversing by
        the shore
musing the inevitable
(yeah, it's a lot to take in)

and it's hard not to drown in imaginings that travel by
        swarm
after 40 days of rain
time enough to plot or surrender to an eternity where clouds
        continue emptying

plagues and pestilence turn your hummings into staccatos
only to be distracted by a cicada circling

what if you're given earbuds
wirelessly receiving decibels from wings that flutter a love
        call to every creature
(those caterpillars kicked back after all)
each note floats high above the idling engine of a used ark
runs like new but not for sale

no need
some of us are headed to a new garden now
walking
following the Walker on water into the promised garden of
        grace and truth

Fives, Family Trees, and Fungi

Antron, Kevin, Korey, Raymond, Yusef
Advertised as Central Park criminals – part of their
       sentence
Tragedy minus triumph – even in their release

Joe, Martin, Morris, Cyril, Percy
Five of the 50 who mutinied – birthed the Port Chicago
       cemetery
Uniformed for bravery – condemned for its display

Rahab, Ruth, Obed, Jesse, David
Lineage toward salvation – promises fulfilled unexpectedly
Decisions selfish and selfless – merged on a merciful path

Harold, Robert, Charles, Norman, Marie*
Siblings of emergency rooms – by virtue of their colorblind
       hearts
Triaged with ignorance – a pattern of suture, relapse, repeat

Carter, Ernest, Freddie Lee, George, Sam
Penicillin withheld for science's sake – Tuskegee style
       extermination
Vaccine labels now apologize – with print too small to read
Photo album pages catalogue the commonalities:
White snow, white lab coats, white sheets, white soap suds –

reminders
The black ain't what's s'posed to wash off

*The five children of my paternal grandparents Harold and Ivy Lyons.

my friend Hoke

Drove Miz Daisy to the store
Drove his daughter to school
Drove himself to ask for a raise

Only white man's hand he ever shook was Boolie's
And before he learned to read the newspaper, he learned
Pictures can't hide who ain't important

Saw his share of fallen heroes
Like the time he followed Fannie Lou to Atlantic City
Where Adam Jr. asked her to stop singing about freedom

Or the time his thoughts toured the streets of Chicago
The land where William betrayed Fred
Both flawed and tortured and disappointed and needy
            and human

He mourned for Martin, as well as for the dinner he missed
And understood why his invitation arrived too late
And why Martin wasn't allowed to be right and be wrong

But Mr. Coleburn wasn't crushed
He lifted no man so high as to shatter
When gravity kept its promise
The only One so revered
Was the One who gave him dignity

The One who drove him from one Yassuh to another
The One who hired him to say Yassum with pride
The One who invited him to sit up front as a friend

My friend knew the blessing of locusts
Knew one day they'd find out they'd been replaced
With a beauty they couldn't devour

He'd watched the Miz who memorized the back of his neck
Slip into a consciousness where Thanksgiving pie
Tasted better than unbelief

All this I learned when Hoke leaned out the car window
And honored me with a wave – more like a toss
I caught the crumpled paper bag with this note inside:

Be faithful to keep the pantry stocked
With cans of salmon and love

*Note: Hoke, Daisy, and Boolie are the three characters in Alfred Uhry's
1988 Pulitzer Prize winning play* Driving Miss Daisy.

Verse 2

fragmented education

class reunion

schoolbuses are for sissies so he
walked
and without breathing when a softball would threaten
a land within range of either hand
instead dropping uncaught
breaking the thrower's ancestral expectation

do tell him what lineage procreates in white-collar hallways
long
and where pedestrians address him maybe not by virtue of
       his hue
but a truth makes him sweat cold during walks
like a nude bottle holds tight the opposite temperature
since conforming is so un-70s

and for him so unsinister
then the night arrives
when once-upon-a-time classmates turn dancefloor to
       airport

look down this and that runway from standby
thoughts taxied in all directions from 20, 30, 40 years
       prephobia
ah then he walked with Baldwin and Hughes
Ellison, Larsen, and Wright in the doorway handing out

       syllabi
for a course in self-aviation
after missing decimals, fractions, the meaning of trig
mastering neither the grounder nor the flyball always
       blocking the sun
from lighting the cloud pointing home

now he studies apples
how many can one seed hold

Career moves

Harlem I never knew
you renaissanced my mind
in images of manic-borne masterpieces.
No sense recreating. My debt to you is paid
in library fees
video rentals
book store hours measured in increments of a legacy.
Abyssinian walls I have touched but time
had robbed them of their power to reconcile
Langston and Zora.
Fingers and flappers were
so, so in vogue a mere two score and six before
I was
a teacher's pet practicing black power proverbs
under my breath until I learned/admitted I was yellow.
So symbolic/so inevitable:
the human heart's tainted phlegm/my family's history of
            stapled sternums.
Do Harlem doctors know something I don't?
All I want is to see if the shoe fits.

Raining on my parade

Whoever heard of a parade with only three floats?
In between each
the horses and motorcycles trample the confetti
made with blank love notes
to the neighbors in the houses across the street.
No band, no music, no breath to make the notes
turn into sounds.

First there's Pollyanna.
But she looks surprisingly sad.
Maybe because she's waving from behind protective glass.
She wants to face death's countenance in the crowd
but no one believes she cares.

Second is Poison.
But he looks happy and contented
as a last-minute entry.
Maybe because incarnate sermons have been banned
from the public square
by popular demand for a more imperfect, intolerant
way of life.

Third is Presence.
But this one is empty.
Only those who sit on the curb can see

there are bodies beneath the carriage
and blood on the wheels.
As if it was the only place Jimmy Lee Jackson
and James Reeb and Viola Liuzzo
could share their laughter on a bridge
could share their selves with one another.

Whoever heard of a parade with only three floats?
Who knew three branches of government
wouldn't be enough to remind the crowd how to speak
to themselves tired of every pain turning into a protest
and oh so weary of every marriage to a march?
Sound-off; 1, 2; sound-off; 3, 4…
The cadence pulsing louder than the sirens and sobs.

Perhaps a summer storm can cool off the pavement
at least.
Soaking the Shoulders upon which the government is yet
            to rest.
And at the end of the day
only tire marks got televised.
There just weren't enough floats.

Note: In memory of three who lost their lives before and after the march across the Edmund Pettus Bridge, so that the journey from Selma to Montgomery would not be in vain.

Empathy

Frankenstein was my friend
The monster, not the doctor
What, did I just call my friend a monster?
All he wanted was to be loved by his inventor
Instead he got pretty burned

If only I had been in the lab
The moment his eyes opened
Could I have convinced him his life mattered?
All the eyes glaring saw only green stitches
A lighter shade than his heart had turned

By the time I rolled up on my skateboard
The windmill's wooden door had been broken
Where is Don Quixote when you need him?
All the quests in the world converged
But failed to reverse the fate of the spurned

Tucked under my arm a matching skateboard
A personalized gift with decals of Oz
Enough to awaken the courage of balance?
From lifetimes spent envying other riders
I doubt he was aware that he yearned

Sitting on a park bench in his memory
Named out of guilt not remorse
Picture us rolling down the bike path?
All the signage prohibits compassion
No one dare feign a hint of concern

It's time I face the sails of that windmill
Let my imaginary friend go to sleep
What about the monster that I am?
All my seeking to know Love's inventor
Who bore eons of hate yet un-learned

Tuesday at the Library

Be aware another black man has entered the room.
Still nervous after all these years when kinfolk arrive
And sense soul food recipes scarcely scented on my breath.
Know what else?
That if we are caught reading the same books then
I had better have an answer that satisfies security as to who I
Am on Wednesday through Monday.
God knows I forget who I really want to please.

Image bearers

storyteller perched
on a garbage can   actually beside
despite rancid colors bleeding gums   turn the tide
still
waters of spit spatter glistening between sunset rays
and shame becomes worth the cost of 10 minutes at the end
of a once upon a hot summer day

listener
sits in a trance   or is one
gagged by lack of suspicion or excess guilt
to hear an episode of hardship spewing such filth from pages
turned by moistened lips that have kissed fate breathless
     times
and swallowed skin in mouthfuls chapped from constructing
     each scene
but weaker than shoeless toes kick at his-and-hers dreams

storyteller proceeds
entertaining himself with lyrics of heroics   versus the virus
     he spreads
yawning the refrain
in perfect pitch describing water crashed against rocks that
are his lover's cheeks
leaving so much pain for weeks obscured by dead prose
     of life with a GED

how it groans through their guts to pass
to be

listener
surrenders in God we trusts
enough to make up the forty cents short of a bus ride back
        to the shelter
almost like home for storyteller's collection of sharpened
        number twos
in case he should choose to tell stories on paper bags and
        blues instead
but studios charge
by the hour

A Tale of Two Pauls

Mr. Dunbar
High school classmate of Orville Wright
Operated an elevator
Wrote of bests and worsts; ups and downs; flights and falls;
      and masks

Mr. Apostle
Pupil of Gamaliel
Stitched tents for pitching
Wrote of a far better rest; despairs and hopes; deaths and
      lives; and asks

Related perhaps
By a common ancestor or descendant; friend or foe; Author
      or armor; or wound

Overlooked perhaps
By those whose hearts are too masked or ambitions too
      tasked; or untuned

Pre-Chorus 1

the Talk continued:
when a white person says
(parts 1-3)

When a white person says, "I want the same respect that you're asking of me."
Your emotions may say, "So you're offering conditional love. You can keep it."

But my Father says, "I demonstrated My love like this: while you were still a sinner, My Son died for you. Receive that love and share it." [1]

When a white person says, "Look, I found a black person who thinks like me and talks like me and agrees with my political views and biblical interpretations – this black person gets it."
Your emotions may say, "So what you really want is for the world to be white, like you."

But my Father says, "If you love those who love you, what's your reward? If you greet only your brothers and sisters, what's extraordinary about that? Be like My Son." [2]

When a white person says, "But…."
Your emotions may say, "So you've chosen not to hear my pain."

But my Father says, "But let none of these things move you; nor count your life dear to yourself, so that you may finish your race with joy, and the ministry which you received from your Messiah, My Son, to testify to the gospel of My grace." [3]

Chorus 1
What Color Blood?

(a letter from Nathan)

Dear Mama,

This is my third letter to you in the past week, but so many things have happened that I want you to know. And it gives me more chances to practice my writing. Mostly I want to thank you for all the things you told me back on the plantation. I have found them to be true. "Let God be true and every man a liar." I still remember those words you repeated over and over from the book of Romans. When I asked you what color blood was the enemy's, you told me God's truth. Today I am a witness that secessionist blood is the same color as mine.

It is also the same color blood as Daniel's. He is the one I wrote you about before, the one who showed up at camp with stories of his escape from the old Creek plantation down the way. 'Tis a mystery how we never crossed paths until now. Well Mama, I just laid Daniel in the ground with all my heart and dreams and planning we done for our futures in freedom. His last words were of a girl named Essie. I have not forgotten what you told me about grief and how joy comes in the morning. I am waiting for that joy.

Photographers pass through here regular, so I am sending a picture card of me and Daniel taken just yesterday, right before he was shot. The Johnnys like to scare us with a few shells every time we start to relax. One of them flew right through Daniel's chest and into the tree he was leaning against while he was snoring so peaceful. All the soldiers wants pictures to send to their loved ones at home. I know not exactly where I am, except that it is only a quarter-hour walk to the town over a grassy ridge. Yet you know how fast I walk, so it might take somebody else a whole hour. Captain says for me to walk over at dusk to spy and make sure no rebel soldiers are left there. Makes a man feel important, going from slave, to runaway, to cook, to spy. I want to be a good spy, Mama, not like the ones I read about who came back to Moses full of fear and fright. I wonder what color was Moses. Color seems such an important thing. You know my favorite color is still green, like the little pine needles from the majestic trees.

Here is the picture, Mama. Daniel paid for a copy with some coins he took out a dead rebel's pocket. That is when I saw the blood. What do you think of the picture - have I changed? We got none of your pork gravy here in camp. I try to make the coffee strong enough to soften the tack so our teeth don't break off. I got those strong teeth like you say your Daddy had. I do stay strong, Mama. I get along fine, I assure you. So far, the soldiers in these tents here are the friendliest ones I can recall, even the officers. One of them let me wear his hat for the picture. Now that they got colored troops, maybe I should join up. I have yet to come across one, but Daniel did and he say some of them say they was born free. Mama, I am learning what freedom can be like. Just being me and not fearing I am too small to live. I guess Daniel found

39

freedom already. I still wonder about David. It makes my insides twist and turn to think that we are fighting against each other, when all we did was play together until we old enough to know our place.

Looks like I write a long letter, Mama. It might be the last one for a while since I got special duties now. I owe it to David and Amelia that I can read and write. Even some of the soldiers struggle how to sound out words. Maybe one day I can help teach them. I know you would like that, Mama. I think God would like it too. Thank Mrs. Reynolds for reading this letter to you. Keep on watching and praying.

Your loving son,
Nathan

Verse 3
facing the pain

variations on a Christmas Carol

slapped in the face and kicked in the core
the radio announced the election results
limbs sank into the mattress
then snatched by hands attached to a white hood
eyes ablaze through homemade holes
throat clutched so I cannot speak
I hear my love praying for me
as my host flies me to a tree with a rope
no it's a church

hoods of all colors bowed reverently
next moment raised angrily
organ pedals hum a familiar song
from this view, a boat run aground in the distance
boarded by chained passengers
singing the same song but with deafening dissonance
I hear my brother praying for me
as my host points me to a plank
no it's a bus

the driver and tour guide and bomber are one
telling of his pillaged soul

bruises like imprints of chains across his face
barefoot and sack clothed and weeping
beautiful words amputate hate
hoods blow off, ropes unravel, chains become dust
I hear a prayer from Golgotha
as my host tucks me back into bed
no it's heaven

White Supremacy
to the Tune of Tommy

Some call it a hoax
Some call it a horror
Some thrive from it
Some die from it

The voices of four little bombed black girls
Silenced
The bloggings of more bombastic pundits
Amplified

Are statistics traced to the logo on the letterhead?
Are blood types deciphered by the location of the lab?

Are analyses owed to the speed of the flipper?
Are replays aimless balls of confusion with a jab?

Some hear an agenda on the left (ding)
Some sense a strategy on the right (dong)
Some see colorless, genderless chalk lines (game over)
Some call it deaf, dumb, and blind – and ask –

Why is it easier to play pinball than to love the player?

We Don't All Scream

There's an ice cream named after a man who knelt
tanning-booth complexion and hair soft like felt.

Crackers and chocolate swirled together with ease
but outside the container consumers will tease.

What does justice taste like? don't think while you eat.
Enjoy scoops of indifference, melting ever so discreet.

To endure the freezing headache doesn't have to be scary
and for the intolerant ones, it's even non-dairy.

Elevator Ride

In the time in takes to go from floor one
to floor thirty-four
a half-dozen humans sneak
eight AM glimpses of their reflections
in the shiny door while it seals
off all questions about a jealous running back
justified.

Opinions don't matter now
that he is free and I'm nearly suffocating
from this atmosphere of assumptions
since jokes about dark gloves and blanco broncos
are lost on me, the one so shamed
for not watching the proceedings.

Now I'm watching glow-in-the-dark numbers
as each floor passes by like a bus station
and we're the freedom riders of the north
but we're standing apart when the doors open
and I imagine someone stepping
into a lobby filled with fountains and facilities
unlabeled and with patrons
who wash their own clothes.
And on this ride
most of the collars are white and the necks

concealed in contrast to my beige-on-beige
though I might as well be wearing
hand-stitched overalls
(a little skill I learned in school).

I'm nobody's farmer yet I know
the plow can be more painful
the more fallow the ground
as it kicks around pieces of dirt
and wardrobes get determined by what's clean
in the closet.

So I keep imagining that everyone but me
washes their laundry in private
or at least in laundromats where no one sits
on the tables and the clothes fold
themselves and the fan blows purified air
from blades that spin silently thus inviting
conversations to be carefully taut.

All the used softener sheets find their way
to the trash can and the trash can
is emptied on the hour by
the last one who used it and all around
are attorneys who know how verdicts are vended
and which unmentionables
to drip dry on display.

Oh how attitudes change over time
and with the right legal incentives
that overrule the glares that accuse me
of celebrating in slave cabins all night.

But where was the Spirit
and when was the point of repentance
that ushered in an era of welcomed jubilees?

Was it while I was imagining?

If only I had taken time to interview everyone
including me: "Why does it matter so much
what they think?"

I'll save that for the ride at noon.
Oh now I'm late and I missed my floor!
Time to go backwards and ride some more.

Net Worth

From an oak-top view, my wingspan felt doubled
Set to soar across ranges where skyscrapers tour
While my heart beat like a snare drum of war

I've descended from those that found a home in the Temple
Like swallows nest safely where worshippers seek rest
While my heart beat like a conga in my chest

My ancestors heard first-hand of their half-penny lives
Yet even their plummet was worth their Founder's care
While my heart beat like a stick to a snare

Fellow sparrows trill and fall without waking
Having known human life is worth more than their own
While my heart beat like a tom with no tone

Songs sung when Hosea bought back Gomer
Bounced across seas…one wave at a time
To a land where Elaine and Tulsa held auctions
Currency shaped into curses that rhyme

Nations get to choose what they do and don't stand for
Me? I have nothing to spin or to hide (like Katyn)
While my heart beat like a djembe again

Then at 38th and Chicago a man's life was assessed
I shook cheeping and chirping to get a closer look
While my heart beat like an un-lathed cymbal that shook

I heard clearly the second his lungs stopped expanding
When an officer's pocket became a holster for hate
While my heart pounded like timpani of fate

I know Who saw first and cried before it happened
But I leaned over too far - now I'm looking up from the grass
While my feathers blow lifeless
While my beak blocks the breeze
While our brown faces lose their brightness
While our heart beats both freeze

A Day at the Zoo

Oooh, Mommy, what kind of creature is that?
I've never seen one in this habitat before.

> *It's alright to whisper the epithets – I don't think it can*
> *hear you.*
> *But use a friendly tone just in case.*

Oh, look, there's a bandage wrapped around its neck. What
happened to it?

> *That's a necktie, dear; but don't get too close – you*
> *might touch its hair.*
> *They don't like to have their hair touched.*

Oooh, Mommy, can I come back tomorrow?

> *I think you've seen enough.*
> *You can read about this creature at home where it's safe.*

But I saw a baby one in the backyard next door.

> *Oh my, the new neighbors. Maybe the nice parents*
> *adopted it.*
> *I'll be sure to stop by and introduce myself.*

Can I visit the lions before we go?

> *Honey, not here. Anyway, this is their nap time.*
> *They're probably asleep.*

And you said "Bring Your Child to Work Day" would be boring.

say their names

I can't say their names
I just can't
then I would have to attend their funerals
I would have to sign the guest list
and their loved ones would know my name
and my address

then I would have to forgive their enemies
and know *their* names
since they would be my enemies too
but I can't bear to have *that* many enemies
I can't forgive *that* much

I can't grieve that much
I can't weep that much
I can't deny that much

or can I?

my King decreed me guiltless
the one who was His enemy
and murdered many with my anger
though they didn't die and didn't know me
but they mattered to Him

because His kingdom is love
where He knows *every* name
even mine
and He attends my funeral daily
where I die to the me

the me who forgets
my real name

Pre-Chorus 2

the Talk continued:
when a white person says
(parts 4-6)

When a white person says, "You got your black president. What more do you want?"
Your emotions may say, "You got your 45 white presidents. Isn't that enough?

But my Father says, "I know how to humble those who walk in pride. I know how to give grace to the one who trembles at My word. Have the mind of My Son. For I do not see as man sees; I look at the heart" [4]

When a white person says, "Don't hold me responsible for what my ancestors did!"
Your emotions may say, "Then don't hold me back for what my ancestors endured – and don't live off the privilege they provided!"

But my Father says, "I will not be mocked. What was sown

will be reaped. Remember, your inheritance is undefiled and unfading; your citizenship is with Me. For what do you have that you did not receive?" [5]

When a white person says, "We need to get back to when America was great."
Your emotions may say, "Back when America was great at what? Pledging allegiance or defending bigotry?"

But my Father says, "There is a way that seems right to a man, but in the end it is the way of death. I have shown you what is good — to do justice, love mercy, and walk humbly with Me." [6]

Chorus 2
What Color Blood?

(a letter from David)

Dearest Mother,

May this letter find you and Mammy safe, if only with the comforts of good health and company in this time of war. You would not like this sight, but you would rather know the truth. Our enemy thus far has left the town untouched by torch or canon, but they have killed most of my company. The wounded we have dragged into the courthouse building, where they are all arranged on the floor, staring at the sanitary walls of justice, which I am sure must mock their crusade. The residents of the town – a mere mile away from the Union camp – have fled, but we have been unable to secure a place for their return. The few blacks that remained we had to shoot, if for no other reason than to keep them for aiding our enemy.

Every time I fired, I thought of Nathan. Despite my best efforts, I cannot deny him as a friend, though my company's every utterance about his race uses terms not befitting a fellow human being. I wonder if he joined one of Lincoln's colonization efforts in Haiti. Perhaps he is making a home for himself in Canada. Perhaps he lies bleeding somewhere on the outskirts of a battlefield. Or perhaps he has been captured and is being mercilessly scourged for exhibiting more intelligence than thought fitting for a man of his complexion. Would I be scourged as well for teaching him to read? What a sight we were, with Amelia teaching him how to write. She was the one whose penmanship was so precise, but I trust you can see that mine has improved. Thank you for supporting my conclusion not to chase or report Nathan after he ran away.

As for your decisions, Mother, I hope you have recovered from your spell of guilt over selling what was left of our place to Uncle Timothy. Let his lot deal with this proclamation of Lincoln's. I talk as if he is our president, when we have Davis to revere. To document any more of my truest feelings toward our so-called liberator would incriminate me. For now, I hide my gratitude for having an excuse to wash our household's hands of slavery. You realize, of course, that we are not the only ones who fled when Lincoln's intentions were made known. Neither can I see us being the only ones glad to receive the news. You are better off on the border, where I hope to join you one day soon.

I was saddened but not shocked to receive your news that Amelia did not join you. I can appreciate how difficult the transition has been, all that you have forsaken, with little more than uncertainty to look forward to. Your son, the well-trained soldier who was promoted to captain, I remind you, must bid farewell and choose whether to attend to the moans of my company or the rustling I detect outside. We have been warned that the Union troops nearby may send a spy to determine how many of us remain and in what condition.

As for Nathan, I console myself with imaginings that he is free. I expect never to know what became of him. I do hope he makes something of himself. It is no secret that he could be a great teacher. He was a great friend, a true one, and a forgiving one. And you are a forgiving Mother, to forbear with a wayward daughter and a complacent son. In the event it is imminent, I dare pray that my death will be a courageous one. Fear not, Mother, for I believe your labors will prove not to have been in vain.

Fondest regards,
Your son David Reynolds

Bridge
fellowship frees

Thanksgiving Feast

God knows what His children need
And feeds them for each day
Sometimes we gorge ourselves on scraps
Still starving til we pray

Arriving to be seated
Impatient, insecure
Our Host asks, "May I help you?"
Are we willing to endure?

While others read the menu
Finding love in every course
Serve, be served, or cower
Or take all we want by force?

But I didn't learn Christ in that way
When I fell is when we met
And on the dish I dropped and shattered
He plates the best meal yet

Parking Lot Prayer Meeting

You never leave my side
Which side?

The side that covets and cringes when called to speak?
The side that revels in revealings – not contrivings – too
   sacred to tweak?

Wait
The car just stopped doesn't matter where
Back seat alone and not driving
Eyes shut heart open mind crawling about time to start
   trusting instead
Aside and in spite of

The side that fears and frets and fumbles when the pass is
   delivered
The side that longs to love and lighten and leave all for a
   soul's sake (I just shivered)

But forsaking the seat belt is my limit
Helpless empty handed as yet unhealed
Til You spin it

Same song, new side and the opposite of alone
This is forever
Aching. Rejoicing. All in one. Two different sides?
Armed with a tissue to fight the tears that surely win
Wrong battle
Just listen
Someone is pleading
Inexpressible groans

From which side?
Inside

summer reading

Untangling Emotions
the title of the book reading me
revealing me
how I got tangled
while sitting plucking flowers
from under a tree

I had a chance to meet
one of the authors
but I stayed in the shadows
in the comfortable shade
where assumptions bloom into a
beautiful bouquet

until you smell it
the stench from not changing
the water in the vase
(since some of the petals were wilted anyway)
not the textures the author would rather display
or so I say to myself on this breezeless day

there on the page I haven't turned to yet
maybe that's me

proof my resemblance
warrants no recoil
seeds of an eternal encounter
embedded in the sequel's soil

but not if I don't introduce myself
wilted, stinky and wistful
before I lose the light to see him sitting too
before he loses sight to see the thanks he's due
before the solstice sets
on our emotions

that Flatbush Avenue feeling

that dreaded-hoped-for command from the pulpit for me
to grope through the soil of my inferiority
or simply extend from somehow my innermost roots
into the earth that protects another life
long enough to implant a greeting there in someone's soul
        one soul here
 and there "God bless you"s are whispered
                        mumbled
                        spoken
                        shouted
with no more meaning than the words that they are but they
        are more
when shaped into
                    a hand

a handshake
with indelible prints that walk up my arm
then drop
and attach a cord around my waist
pulling
around my waist
tighter
around my back and in the background
is that music?

a psalm
I hear a rhythm

                    of palms

palms
pressed through my back
into my spine circulating the current of their selfless lifeline
a signal for my chin to stop at that spot
a few inches above his shoulder blade
where blades of grass (how many?) may have easily
                        (how often?) been crushed
but never more than my jaw is now
now where oh where now my head tilts
would you believe?
on his shoulder for a moment's rest

but what to do with

                    my hands?

don't mention

                    my heart

am I all that

naked
that this holy embrace
arrived to cover my self-consciousness
obstruct my blindness

that convinces me with my eyes closed I am better off
or am I dead?
no not before I am delivered from fear
clutching my throat but my hands I told you (didn't I?)
won't reach there
so I smear my fingers across his back
where my "God bless you" slobbers its way out rolls down
          and evaporates
bypassing my throat and its diary of confessions for trying
to act unswollen

                              my throat

screaming wake up

but the fear is gone that fear of everything of even waking up
except the fear of looking into his eyes the eyes where it all
          started there
before I was looking into or outof
overwhelmed not understanding
they're standing still there wherever
                         and even
                         when
                         I was shown to my pew even
                         and when
                         I recall my wanderings

wondering what a spectacle I was
wearing so many colors from so many miles away
with so many secrets light and
       secrets dark and
       near and far all converging
            attacking and
            suffocating and
            exploding
            into

                his arms

arms
that raised the church on Flatbush into a place of praise
praise
that raised me out of my soil my secrets my seat
long enough to receive what was commanded

for our next appointment

what if you took up the wrong cross?
what if you took on the wrong yoke?
what if you're denying the wrong self?
what if you're sowing to the wrong spirit?

"what if I really love you?
"what if I really advocate for you?
"what if I really want you with Me?
"what if I'll be here waiting...when you return"

Forty-Six

I need a refuge
I need a refuge from myself
I need a refuge from the noise
of the mountains being cast into the midst of the sea
of the nations raging with their chariots of greed
of the tantrums of disappointment wailing inside of me

I need a declaration
I need a declaration of dependence
I need a declaration of dawn's gladness to replace
the spears of false accomplishment being hurled overhead
the threat of indecision and visions of dread
the unbelief in a Presence here to break by fears instead

I need a psalm

This Is the Day

Permission
hangs like a willow branch
reachable
but not strong enough to hold any weight

Rejection
chokes like a sip of water
thirst-quenching
but going down the wrong way

Elation
rises like rays peeking past the horizon
promising
but interrupted by a stratus-full day

Progression
like a shoulder tap in a crowd
inviting
but down the Dolorosa trail

Chorus 3
What Color Blood?

(a letter from Amelia)

Dear David,

Are you surprised to receive a letter from me? Truthfully, you are my last resort. My letters to our Mother, and then to Nathan's mother, have gone unanswered. I am desperate enough to write to the brother whose last words to me were accusations of lasciviousness. I will get to the point.

You recall that the Creek plantation down the road was a source of what you referred to as amusement for me. While you thought, at first, I was aiming to catch the eye of their overseer, next you were convinced I was endangering the life of one of their field hands, Daniel, by spending time there. I was actually teaching Daniel – as we had taught Nathan – to read and write. The desire to teach burned in me so, and seeing Nathan's enthusiastic progress, I wanted to test my skills and expand my usefulness. So, in a sense, I suppose I was endangering him, since I was educating him beyond his legal station.

During the course of my visits, Daniel confided in me that a girl in the slave cabin adjacent to his was carrying his child. He was terrified. She was not yet visibly with child, unless one's glance lingered. He feared that when her state was discovered, one of two outcomes would befall them. Either the master's wife would accuse her husband of fathering the child, considering his visits to the quarters and his previous transgression. Or the master himself would be enraged that someone else got to her first. Either way, Daniel was convinced that he and Essie would be separated.

Had we possessed the means, and had I the imagination to concoct a believable reason, I would have asked Father to purchase her, for her own protection and so her child would at least be in the vicinity of its father. Yet, everything happened so fast. The proclamation to free the slaves, Father's decree to dissolve everything, his passing, Nathan's decision to leave before he was granted papers, then you running off to war, Mother selling everything to Uncle and moving north with Mammy. It was all too much.

Yes, brother, I realize I have not yet gotten to the point. Essie birthed her child – a fine, though sickly boy. She had yearned to marry Daniel and raise their child together in the fear of God. Alas, she breathed her last during childbirth. I was with her, posing as her owner as we traveled north, apart from Mother and Mammy. She had chosen the name Daniel if he was to be a boy. Now, here I am, with a Negro baby to care for. Thankful that he was born free, and not knowing how to reach his daddy.

What do I ask of you? Find Nathan, and, through him, find Daniel. Even as I write this, I know the impossibility. Yet, since Daniel ran away only a few days before Nathan, and since their escape likely took a similar path, it is conceivable that they connected. Or perhaps you could write to Mother and ask her to intervene. As beside myself as I am, my faculties are directing me toward prayer for God to intervene.

You see, David, those Bible verses that Nathan used to repeat have stayed with me, and I have begun attending a congregation led by a minister who was influenced by a Rev. Josiah Henson, a former slave from Maryland. Perhaps there is a day, a place where we might all reunite and even walk together on the road, a place where you can put away your weapon and Nathan can stop running. After all, our blood is the same color. I have heard that Rev. Henson has a settlement in Canada, which I intend to visit. Perhaps I can be of some use in providing education to the emancipated. It seems a good place for little Daniel to grow up.

Your sister, Amelia

Outro

falling forward

Postcards from Bob

What was it like in Korea?
Did you stack the bodies six high, like Doub* did?
Or were you next to six corpses rotting until the skirmish
        silenced
and the ammunition cooled?
Doub was from Pittsburgh. Maybe your companies kept
        company?
I mean, did they keep all you colored men together?
Or did you stand out—like on your high school basketball
        team?
And not for your jump shot.

Maybe that's why you tickled me as soon as you got home
        from work.
So you could hear a laughter you missed until the barracks?
Or to return to the laughter you'd heard before but not
        since?

Too many questions? Well, I never received a post card.

Maybe you never sent one.
Too painful to write what you saw?
Or you didn't want me to grow up and cower any more than

        I did
at the thought of your prowess in battle.
What did you do to earn those service medals I saw
        pictured?
Did they make you proud or conflicted?
Is that why you wanted me to be on the honor roll at school
and learn to do my own laundry at home?
How many times did you wash your uniform?
How many times did you fill your canteen?

Who was there to greet you when you stepped off the plane
        back home?
Sadly, not your departed mom. One of your brothers?
Or your dad, who had worn a uniform some three decades
        before?
You left me no shoebox with all the treasure—the artifacts
        of what the angels saw.

Tell the nameless one to write me,
the one who protected you, so you could tickle me more and
        more.

*Korean War veteran in August Wilson's play *Jitney*

get over it

cardinal's song
just the grace note released without exhaling sends
no carries you to the grave
where grandma's remains are quiet next to those of your
heart
tree-shaded
so the slightest breeze awakens summer desires
aural hot and pressing in on your chest's pulse racing
then stilled
by jubilation of ice cubes escaping into glassed-in water
and stilled again
as if she shared a cherished sip
and again
each time you twist and untwist your neck so one eye at least
can espy the red-throated master of the only voice from the
skies
grandma taught you to recognize

other than God's

she's gone
get over it
sanguine solicitors can cure you with their need for paper

faces from your pocket
the pleading voices of nameless pseudo-siblings
whom you resent for smiling more brightly than she did
are they hearing you/me crying for them?
bargained restitution for when I was four and chased half a
block the black bullies
self-sanctified buckler for the neighbor I knew not as white
just thought could be taught to reach up from Down's
to the cardinal's notes now I want silenced for all ears

other than God's

no other gods can have me circa June-July
when noonish shall hear me crying curses at Lincoln
Cemetery's folding chairs
fully or maybe in ignorance empty of homage due her
52 years alone dear widow
I grieve they excluded a plane ride
resting under leaves at root-side I'll resume my lament
pray for even pigeons she smiled at
these many months ignored and unfed but I can't point
not polite she taught
them to her ashes
so how is it He points me over there under that Tree where
I'm over it for now
anoints me to wake up content to be a grandson
not a cardinal

Arrival

Ready for the rocking chair
Earned, purchased, bestowed, or bequeathed?

Underneath the porch listen to the souls speak
Rock gently lest wisdom is drowned out by the creaks

Sink back into the weight of the years
Let the broom rest in the corner after sweeping the tears
Flushing out the dirt from the road of no more fears

The hours pass peacefully in the rocking chair
Even if no one is listening

The glistening of voices has a timbre that's delicate
Forgetful, yet hummable—simple, yet intricate

Still trying to obtain what was already given?

let go of the bottle

a trickle from your tear duct
a dribble from your nostril
a droplet in the corner of your mouth

easy to wipe away
easy to sniff away
easy to dab away

gone are the shards of glass
gone are the fragments of if onlys
gone are the overcompensating bleeds

until the wound reopens
until the enemy reappears
until the weapon resumes

its journey from generation to generation
its trajectory from temple to rubble
its path from perchance to permanence

waiting in line at the entrance
waiting at the entrance to be served
waiting to serve those in line

to the degree they'll allow you
to the degree you treasure their glance
to the degree you deem yourself clean

you can only reach an arm's length
you can only offer what you've received
you can only walk where light is

some roads never get paved
some hinges never get oiled
some bandages never get unwrapped

even though you've studied
even though you've prayed
even though you've practiced

every sniffle serves a purpose
every tissue tries to last
every tear has a bottle

kept safe only by the Father
kept unknown until its time
kept healed forever

homage

A word that roars
Reverbs through thick jungles where skin is transparent
And bruises from dis-compassionate words
But protected by an edifice of vines swaying but immovable
Joined by and for
Ever
Even now
A relative is recognizable by smooth teeth and sharp eyes
A quick paw pulls and pushes to and from
Without dirtying the den
Without disturbing other species
Always mindful of the protective vines
Lest a cub wanders through and falls prey
So many camouflaged hunters aim to muzzle our roar
Into a purr of complacency
It'll take more than darts to tranquilize this legacy
Even though vulnerability is sacrificed
The fittest survive to roar another day
Aching inside for salvation

Spring Fever

Each robin's chip dances
Vaudeville notes piercing open pores
Curtains pulled back
By the breeze that applauds
Enough to soften the imagined splinters
The park bench's contribution to a failed audition
Prisoner of war in a dungeon treehouse
All because someone else found a fresh start.

Someone else's debut broadcast alive from their prison.
No sense waiting for rusty chains to ripen.
Can I, too, rehearsing impromptu lines
Live to see goose bumps absorb a campfire's warmth
Underneath the moonlight where no rain can leak?
Still, splinters can sink deeper.
By now pruned skinless;
Each bird in the wings tapping accusations.

A postlude in the park entitled:
Why so afraid to look up?

send out the clowns

it's rich   creating a new language
usurping vocabulary
redefining opportunity
scorn used to warrant inquiry
sleep walkers used to be awakened or at least
given pillows to land on
not to trip over
a woke was a relief

but now

don't bother   we don't all want the same ending
or is it   we don't know what to ask for
to get what   we really want.

a refund.

are we done?

what about sacrifice   the cross to be taken up
like forbearing the emptiness of the time
that someone
isn't there?
nobody's fault

suppose we try accepting Who's been there all along
next year included
then we won't need any antics
to replace the pain or recover the props.

try a day with entrances only
and improv that's farce free
untethered to anyone's applause.

it's not over
Douglasses still orate and Garrisons still recruit
where did their friendship go?
depends on whose promptings are loudest
and the timing

keep the door open   in case
the curtain call doesn't go as rehearsed
careful not to laugh too soon

Vamp

Birthday Breezes

When 60 comes, go stand at the river.
See how calm.
If you had come 30 years ago, mist
from the rapids would have
stung your face. You could've
ridden them then.
If you come back 30 years later, the
waters might be dried up – though
your skin would crave the moisture
even more.
All you got is today to stand at the
river. Be glad you are standing. Be
glad it's a river, not an ocean. You
doubt? Because you can't see the
other shore? Step into the water.

Ha – and you thought you were on
the other side.

Worth the Wait

it wasn't	as if	dry tear ducts suggested you're healed
it wasn't	as if	a clean plate signaled you're full
it wasn't	as if	the restaurant brandished a new menu
it wasn't	as if	snow-stained windows interrupted the fun
it was	as if	my fireside sessions had been recorded
it was	as if	a mirror not a voice gracefully spoke
it was	as if	after twenty-and-then-some years in the kitchen
		and our Father served an entrée of hope

dust and ashes

for You
O Lord
the most frustrating task
all I ask
is that You hold the sun the right distance to illumine and
the moon close enough to turn my memory of the dark

the mountains tall enough to scratch the star that itches
while
the sea holds its breath until it kisses the shore
all I bear
the quest to paint without numbers
O man
isn't for you

afterword

Zachary "Zach" Dombrowski

Steve...
my brother, my friend, a spiritual father, my co-laborer
in Christ.

My deep appreciation for the love and boldness expressed
through this book.

My heart is deeply stirred by your courage and vulnerability
shared throughout the movements of this composition.

Reaching through the works on each page...
My heart is listening to the healthy tension in feelings of
lament and trusting in God's promise.

I hear the harmony of God's love in your journey.

I see the reconciliation with God as He calls you into empowerment toward self and others.

I experience your receiving redemption so that you're free to be a father.

This indeed stirs deeply that your journey matters. That all the events in your life have purpose. That this journey of revelation is meant to be expressed with the world for God's glory.

We water and plant, God provides the growth.

notes

Pre-Chorus 1

1. Romans 5:8
2. Matthew 5:46-48
3. Acts 20:24

Pre-Chorus 2

4. Daniel 4:37; Isaiah 66:2; Philippians 2:5; 1 Samuel 16:7
5. Jeremiah 14:20; Galatians 6:7-8; Hosea 10:12; 1 Peter 1:4; Philippians 3:20; 1 Corinthians 4:7
6. Proverbs 14:12; Micah 6:8

(a letter from Nathan)
Two Brothers in Arms. United States, None. [Between 1860 and 1870] [Photograph] Retrieved from the Library of Congress, https://www.loc.gov/item/2002719397/.

(a letter from Daniel)
Rees, C. R., photographer. Unidentified young soldier in

Confederate infantry uniform. United States, None. [Between 1861 and 1865] [Photograph] Retrieved from the Library of Congress, https://www.loc.gov/item/2012649108/.

(A letter from Amelia)
Unidentified Woman Sitting With Her Arm Resting on a Table., None. [Between 1860 and 1870] [Photograph] Retrieved from the Library of Congress, https://www.loc.gov/item/2010648883/.

He put **a new song** in my mouth, a song of praise to our God. Many will see and fear, and put their trust in the LORD.

Psalm 40:3 (ESV)

Oh, sing to the LORD **a new song**! Sing to the LORD, all the earth. Sing to the LORD, bless His name; proclaim the good news of His salvation from day to day. Declare His glory among the nations, His wonders among all peoples.

Psalm 96:1-3 (NKJV)

And they sang **a new song**, saying, "Worthy are You to take the scroll and to break its seals; for You were slaughtered, and You purchased people for God with Your blood from every tribe, language, people, and nation.

Revelation 5:9 (NASB)